Poems and More

by fred berri

fred berri

Poems and More
© 2021 frederic dalberri
ISBN: 979-8-9855923-3-7 Print
ISBN: 979-8-9855923-4-4 Ebook

Poems and more...
by fred berri

Contents

Dedication

***

To my grandson, Carmelo
Dreams can come true.
It's up to you.

Ci vediamo quando ci vediamo. See you when we see each other.
Love, Poppy

"Cogito, ergo sum."
"I think, therefore I am"

René Descartes (1596-1650)

Poems

Dreams

© *fred berri*

Day dreams
Night Dreams
Dreams can come true
Dreams that you dream
It can happen to you

What will you do
With the dreams you dream
Will you own a Lamborghini
You can't ask a Genie
We know that won't work

We can't rest on our laurels
You must plow ahead
Dreams can come true
No one knows best
It's all up to you

My Rose

© *fred berri*

There is rose that grows
in my special garden.
No one knows about my rose
or my special garden.
So, allow my pardon
I don't expose my special Rose.

My Butterfly

© fred berri

Butterfly kisses
And all your wishes,
I hope will never be denied.
But life gets in the way
when making plans
Don't let them fade and hide.

How I ponder

© fred berri

When I ponder
And I wander, in my minds eye.
I often wonder of the stars
and the sky.
What will be my legacy
only time will let us see

Waves

Waves in the Ocean.
Waves of emotion.
Waves of good-bye.
Waves of memories that have slipped on by.
Waves of hello to brighten your future.
Waves that never come that are on the fly.
Waves in our thought.
Waves that are naught.
Waves in your life.
Waves that you fought.
Waves that never end is the wave of our flag,
a wave that we will always be able to brag.

Flutter

© *fred berri*

Butterflies flutter, flutter, fly around.
Flutter, flutter, above the ground.
From here to there not to know.
Why it does, to make things grow.

Blue Sails

© fred berri

Blue sails and an ice cream moon
Paints a love tune
That of passion
Always in fashion
Until that love becomes your assassin.

Pain

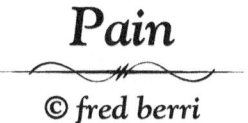

© fred berri

Pain has shown me to believe
Pain has shown me to achieve
Pain delivered me from misery
Pain has shown me my delivery.

Desert Flower

© fred berri

To gaze upon her wonder
Give thoughts of plunder
That awakens the sweet fragrance
Of the Desert Flower
The sweet dessert of a Rose.

and more...

Take a Message Western Union

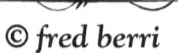

© fred berri

Take a message Western Union
Message to my wife
Tell her that I miss her, I can't stand the single life
I had things going, right in my hand
Now I've got nothin' I'm a lonely man

Take a message Western Union
Message to my wife
California's not the place to straighten out your life
I did not find gold or silver I could touch
The treasure I did find, was in you I miss so much

Take a message Western Union
You've heard it all before
The Teletype is printing, the words she can't ignore
I had things goin', right in my hand
Now I've got nothin', I'm a lonely man

Western Union help me if you can

Take a message Western Union
Message to my wife
Tell her that I threw away the best part of my life
I did not find gold or silver I could touch
The treasure I did find, was in you I miss so much

Western Union help me if you can

Together One More Time

© fred berri

As we lay here, me and you
Where our dreams of love come true
In these magic moments so divine
You take me high as I want to be, wrapped in ecstasy

One more time and I'll be there
One more time with love to share
Just to hear you whisper, darlin' I will always love you

Lay your head down on my shoulder
Let your heart beat next to mine
We'll make music as our passions climb

As the night time fades away
And we face a brand new day
Feels so good to be together, One more time

One more time and I'll be there
One more time with love to share
Just to hear you whisper, darlin' I will always love you

As we lay here, me and you
Where our dreams of love come true
Feels so good to be together, one more time

It's Hard to Describe the Way That I feel

© fred berri

Well, it's hard to describe the way that I feel
But I know that you feel just the same
The feelings inside, we just can't hide
Feelings we masquerade

Well I know that it's true, the feeling in you
I can see it in your eyes
Feelings you have, feelings I see
Feeling we can't disguise

Come take my hand, as lovers do
Let's take our chance for romance
We've got nothing to lose and all to gain
We don't have fortune or fame

But you know what we have, is a feeling of love
A feeling between you and me
A feeling that's right
A feeling that's strong, a feeling that can't be wrong

The dreams that we thought
The plans that we made, are only a heartbeat away

Let's take a chance on these feelings we have
Let's take a chance on romance

I'd Rather Be a Cowboy Than Live in New York City

© fred berri

I'd rather be a cowboy than live in New York City
I'd be ridin' the range instead of the Subway
Seein' the lights of the big white Broadway
I'd be ridin' the range tonight

I thought I'd take a chance and come to New York City
Sing my music all over town
Instead of singin,' it's somethin' else that I found
And I want to go home tonight

There's the hustle of the crowd
And everything's so loud
Lights keep flashin' all night long
There's so much confusion my head's spinnin' round
I can't even sing my song

All my family and friends they'll all understand
The hustle and the gamed I can't comprehend
I'm just a simple folk livin' in New York
I'm packin' my bags I'm gonna make it home

Back to your arms catch the first plane I can
Back to your arms I'll never leave again

I'd rather be a cowboy than live in New York City
I'd be ridin' the range instead of the Subway
Seein' the lights of the big white Broadway
I'd be ridin' the range tonight

My Hero's Have Always Been Cowboys

© fred berri

My Hero's have always been cowboys
I remember my Daddy well
Faded blue jeans n' big buckle belts
Sippin' his long drawn beer

From when I was a little boy
Ridin' on my playschool horse
Wild Bill, Jingles n' Tonto
Roy Rogers, Triger, n' Dale Evans of course

From outlaw to Sherriff, Badrock to barrooms
My Daddy would tell me, Son
When you grow up to be a cowboy
Be a cowboy that's number one

My hero's have always been cowboys
I remember my Daddy well
Ro-day-o's and fairs, stuntmen and movies
Travlin' from here to there

My Daddy would never get tired of takin' me with him right there
The years have gone by to quickly
Now I sit with my son and my beer

My hero's have always been cowboys

The Thunder's Gonna Roll

© fred berri

Our Love is like a thunder storm
Rips the sky apart
Thunder rolls and lightening strikes our two lonely hearts

No matter how we play this game
I'm not gonna lose
So, hold on baby for the ride, I ain't lettin' go

Come on hold me in your arms
Come on hold me, don't let go
Hold on for the ride, the thunder's gonna roll

There's always calm before the storm
Dark before the dawn
Gravity will pull us down, but I keep holdin' on

No matter how we play this game, I'm not gonna lose
So hold on baby for the ride, I ain't lettin' go

We keep on fightin' for our love
Hangin' on by threads
One more round, one more punch
Hearts can't take the blows

No matter how we play this game, I'm not gonna lose
So, hold on baby for the ride, I ain't lettin' go

Thunder storms over head
Rain keeps pourin' down
I don't want to prophecy, I don't want to die
No matter how we play this game, I'm not gonna lose

So, hold on baby for the ride, I ain't lettin' go

Without My Man

© fred berri

You look like you just stepped out of GQ magazine
All the ladies turned their head
You just smile and keep on walkin'
You caught a glimpse of what they said

That don't bother you
You take it all in stride
'Cuase you know what you got waitin'
She's always by your side

No more Hollywood nights
You're workin' nine to five
I never knew you'd fall for
All the hoopla and that jive

Of homecooked meals
Late night TV
Holdin' hands at midnight
Oh! Lonesome me

I know I'd give up one year of my life
If I could hold you one more time

Days are easy, nights are insane
Pacin' the floor, heart filled with pain

God only knows how lonely I am
Day after day without my man
And when I can love someone new
Will it be him or will it be you?

It's So Easy Lovin' You

© fred berri

My baby's proud to be Italian
Comes from Mulberry Street
Loves to hear the Opera, usually falls asleep

She don't take no nonsense
Tells you what's on her mind
Lovin' her is easy down on Mulberry Street

My baby works up town
Fancy clothes and restaurants
Takes her clients to Tribeca Grill

But when my baby's back home again
It's so easy lovin' her down on Mulberry Street

Sunday mornin's ain't so fancy
A small café over on Delancy
The New York Times and some convetsation
Makes it easy lovin' her down on Mulberry Street

Let's go to the park, Central that is
Walk around the Zoo
Look at that Koala, cuddly just like you

My baby's got it all together
From head to toe
That's what makes it easy lovin' her down on Mulberry Street

My baby's a born New Yorker
She'll tell you where to go and how to get there
She mingles with the best of them
Kings and Queens I want you to know
Lovin' her is easy down on Mulberry Street

I Remember

© *fred berri*

I remember how we used to plan our get a-ways
I remember how we used to play hide n' seek
I remember how I said; I'll kill a dragon for you
And then you mothers' call would say; it's time to go
And how we'd plan to run away tomorrow

Tomorrow's here and yesterday is gone
How did you fall into someone else's arms
Didn't I kill enough Dragons for you?
Didn't I say; I love you?

I remember how we'd gallop on our playschool horse
And go to school and have show and tell
You'd tell about becoming a princess bride
And how I'd show off with all my pride

And then the teacher said; It's time to go
And how we'd plan to run away tomorrow
Tomorrow's here and yesterday is gone
How did you fall into someone else's arms?

Something happened, I don't know what?
We went our separate ways a lot
You fell for someone else's charms
I settled for someone else's arms

How many times I think of you?
How many times you think of me?
How many times we go to sleep
And pray our soul to keep

Didn't I kill enough Dragons for you?
Didn't I say; I love you?

When I was down

© fred berri

When I was down
You came around
You lifted me up
From down on the ground
And I fell in love with you

I fell for you
And I know
Right from the start
You'd steal my heart
And I fell in love with you

I lost control
Of everything in sight
'Cause you are the one
Holding me tonight

Let's hold on, don't let go
Let's hold on, to what we found
'Cause if there's a moment to treasure forever
It's this moment I found with you

Quotes

© fred berri

"Twist, turn and bend the truth. Now it's fiction." ™

"The good memories always fade first. That's
why the world looks for a villain."
(From: Cousins' Bad Blood-The Take Over)

"Humpty Dumpty was pushed. Do your homework. It doesn't
mean it's true just because you read it or someone said it!"

"The things that come into your life that you don't
chose, makes you who you've become."

"No matter where you go, you'll always be there in body,
soul and mind. You can run, but you can never hide."

"Being immersed in the past can be intoxication to the soul."

"We should offer reading as a special present to our children and never
forced or presented as a chore they must do. We should offer reading as a
special present to their little minds, so each time in their life they pick up
a book to read, they feel they just opened a new gift."

"I believe something special happens when we open a book and read. We
are transformed into a different place and time."

Acknowledgements

* * *

Publisher: frederic dalberri
Cover design by: JudithS Design

Books by fred berri

* * *

Cousins' Bad Blood
Cousins' Bad Blood-The Take Over
Murder on Contadora Island

* * *

Books featuring Homicide Detective Johnny Vero
Ten Cents a Dance
Bullets Before Dawn-Murder in Chinatown
Sabre Blue Society

* * *

Books featuring Lester Caine-Private Eye
Murder on Palm Beach-The Pigpen Cipher

* * *

Books featuring Adventures of Carmelo

The Adventures of Carmelo is a series of children's learning stories. These stories help children understand new adventures, teaching respect, listening, following instructions, to be brave, and that it's okay to be scared when facing a new adventure.

Thank you. I hope you enjoy reading some of my writings.

fred berri

About the Author

***

berri graduated Columbia State University with an online business degree. He volunteered teaching Junior Achievement in the Florida school district and led a volunteer reading program for grades K-3. He has done public speaking and appeared in TV commercials and voice overs. Berri has written numerous murder mysteries and children's books all of which can be found online: fredberri.com--Amazon-- Barnes & Noble—Kindle—Books-a-Million--Nook and Walmart

www.ingramcontent.com/pod-product-compliance
Lightning Source LLC
Chambersburg PA
CBHW020347130626
46549CB00003B/1340